D0966280

WHALE SHARKS

Anne Welsbacher

Capstone Press
MINNEAPOLIS

Printed in the United States of America.

Capstone Press • 2440 Fernbrook Lane • Minneapolis, MN 55447

Editorial Director   John Coughlan
Managing Editor   John Martin
Production Editor   James Stapleton
Copy Editor   Thomas Streissguth

Library of Congress Cataloging-in-Publication Data

Welsbacher, Anne, 1955-
    Whale sharks / by Anne Welsbacher.
      p. cm. -- (Sharks)
    Includes bibliographical references (p.) and index.
    ISBN 1-56065-271-3
    1. Whale shark--Juvenile literature. [1. Whale shark.
  2. Sharks.] I. Title. II. Series: Welsbacher, Anne, 1955-
  Sharks.
  QL638.95.R4W45 1996
  597'.31--dc20   95-7126
                                                CIP
                                                AC

99 98 97 96 95   6 5 4 3 2 1

Table of Contents

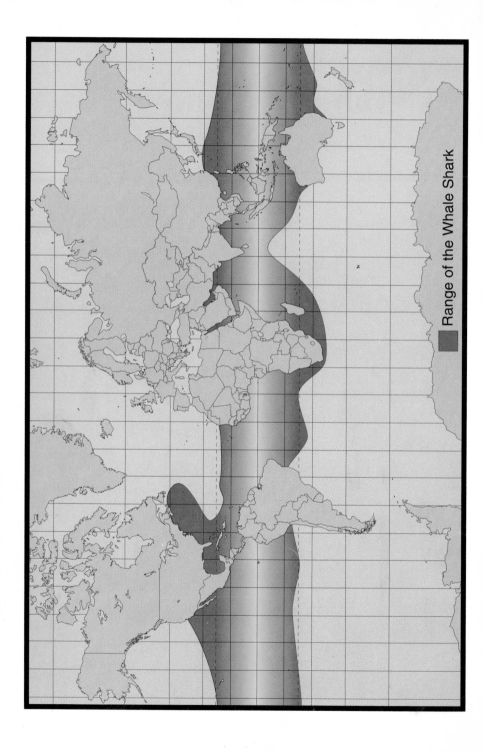

Range of the Whale Shark

Facts about Whale Sharks

Scientific name: *Rhincodon typus*

Closest relatives: The whale shark is the only shark in its family.

Description: The largest shark, named after the whale because of its large size. It has a flat, broad head, with its mouth right at the front of its head, instead of underneath like most sharks. Its mouth is as large as its head. Unlike other sharks, the whale shark lacks a notch at the top of its tail.

Length: Whale sharks average 25 to 35 feet (8 to 10 meters) long. Some whale sharks may reach 50 feet (15 meters) long.

Weight: Whale sharks weigh 8 to 10 tons (7.3 to 9 metric tons).

Color: Dark reddish, brown, or gray on top; white below, with a pattern of yellowish or white spots and stripes on its head, body, and tail.

Food: Small fish and plankton.

Location: Warm waters around the world, in the deep oceans and near land.

Chapter 1

The Biggest
Fish in the Sea

The whale shark is a whale of a fish. The biggest specimens are 40 feet (12 meters) long. Some have been reported as long as 50 feet (14 meters). That's equal to the size of some whales!

Despite their name, whale sharks are not related to whales. Whales are mammals, and whale sharks, like all sharks, are fish.

But whales and sharks do have one thing in common—their huge size. In fact, whale sharks are even bigger than many whales. They are

about the same size as sperm whales and humpback whales.

Car-sized Mouth

You could drive an old Volkswagen into a whale shark's huge mouth. The mouth of a 35-foot (10.7-meter) shark is six feet (two meters) wide.

Even stranger than its size is the location of the mouth. Most sharks' jaws are below their heads. When they bite their prey, the jaws move forward and open wide. But a whale shark is one of the few sharks with a mouth located right at the front end of its broad, flat head.

The mouth opens all the way across the shark's head. So the whale shark can really open wide! All the shark has to do to catch a meal is swim forward. Food tumbles right into the waiting mouth.

Just above the mouth, about four feet apart, are the shark's nostrils. They are right on the front of the head. A slight ridge connects the

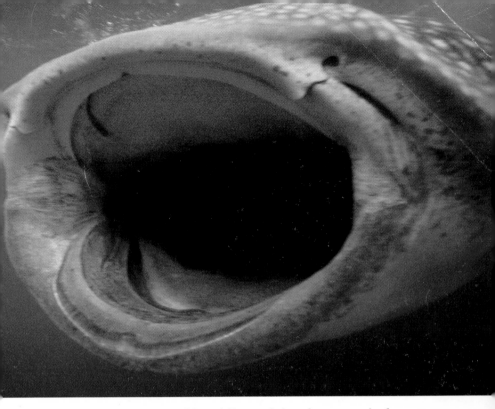

A whale shark opens wide while cruising for a meal of plankton.

nostril and the small eyes on each side of the head.

The Checkerboard Shark

Like most sharks, whale sharks are dark on the top and white below. The dark color has been described as brown, reddish, and dark gray. But what stands out against that dark

Whale sharks enjoy swimming at the surface, but they can dive deep as well.

color is a very unusual pattern of spots and stripes. This pattern does not appear anywhere else in all of nature.

On the big fish's flat head, small, round, white, or yellowish dots are grouped close together. On its back and sides, the spots are larger, more lined up, and more spread out. Rows of stripes and bars, also white or yellowish, separate the spots. The stripes run both across and up and down, like a checkerboard or tic-tac-toe board. Even the tail is spotted.

Nobody knows why the whale shark has this checkerboard pattern of spots. It doesn't need camouflage, which is the usual reason for strange patterns in nature. There is nothing on land or in the sea that a whale shark fears!

Ridges and Tail

The whale shark has three hard ridges running from head to tail on each side of its body. These ridges make the checkerboard pattern stand out even more. The ridges blend into the bigger ridge, called a keel, which strengthens the base of its tail.

When a whale shark takes water into its mouth, it is both breathing and eating. The plankton stays in its mouth, but the water flows

The five gill slits help the whale shark take in oxygen from the surrounding water.

across the gills. The gills remove oxygen from the water just as human lungs remove oxygen from the air. The water then leaves the shark's body through five long openings on its sides called gill slits.

On a whale shark, the gill slits might be two feet (0.6-meter) or more long. But they are not the longest gill slits of all sharks. Basking sharks, the second largest sharks, have gill slits that run down each side and almost meet at the stomach.

A whale shark is the only large shark that does not have a notch near the top of the tail. Scientists don't know why most large sharks have this little chunk missing from the tail. But because it appears on so many different kinds of sharks, they think it must have some function. Or it might have had a function in the distant past.

Many Mysteries

There are many, many things we don't know about whale sharks yet. We don't know how deep the sharks swim. We know almost nothing about how they mate or give birth. We don't even know how long they live.

Whale sharks are very rare. Only about 100 sightings have been recorded. There is no known place on earth where they are common, and no place where they can be studied.

Chapter 2

The Giant Sucking Machine

The biggest shark in the world has teeth so small they are useless. But there are between 3,000 and 6,000 of them! Those teeth are smaller than a fingernail, and not even one-quarter of an inch (6 millimeters) long. Tiny flaps of skin cover the teeth like loose curtains. These teeth grow in 300 long strips or rows.

The huge shark with the huge mouth does not even use its teeth for anything! Instead, it opens up its mouth and simply lets its dinner come to it.

What comes to the shark is mainly plankton, the mass of tiny animals that float in the sea. Plankton is made up mainly of tiny, shrimp-like animals called krill. The whale shark sucks up plankton in huge amounts. Most big whales also eat krill. That's another reason for naming these sharks after whales.

Pursuing Plankton

Whale sharks follow plankton all over the globe as the seasons change. At coral reefs, plankton and other tiny sea creatures can be found swimming in clouds so thick that a diver cannot see through them. They are like thick masses of bubbles floating through the water. A whale shark swims through the cloud with its mouth open, taking in millions of the little creatures.

In other places, a whale shark may find different meals, such as anchovies, sardines, and other fish. It also eats squids and other small crustaceans such as crabs and shrimps, in addition to krill.

A school of anchovies makes a tasty meal for a passing whale shark.

Pumping for Dinner

Sometimes a whale shark feeds another way. It "stands" in the water, its head at the surface and its tail pointed straight down. Then it moves rapidly up and down, like a giant pump.

A diver follows a whale shark as a group of golden pilot fish leads it along.

This movement sucks food right into the shark's mouth, like a giant vacuum cleaner.

Whale sharks have been seen pumping in the middle of schools of tuna. Sometimes big tunas get sucked right in. But no one knows whether the shark actually eats the big fish or not.

A Strange Journey

After a whale shark's dinner has gone into its mouth, the food moves on into the shark's throat. The whale shark's throat is unlike anything found in other fish. Between the gills are crisscrosses of hard tissue called cartilage. This cartilage is covered with a spongy matter.

The spongy material acts like a sieve, or strainer. It lets the water pass out through the gill slits but holds in the plankton and the little fish.

From the throat, the shark's food moves into the stomach. It gets pushed there by the gallons of plankton-filled water that slosh in every time the shark takes another mouthful. That is every 20 seconds or so.

If a whale shark swallows something it can't digest, it takes care of the problem very simply. It turns its stomach inside out! When the problem food is gone, the stomach slides back into place.

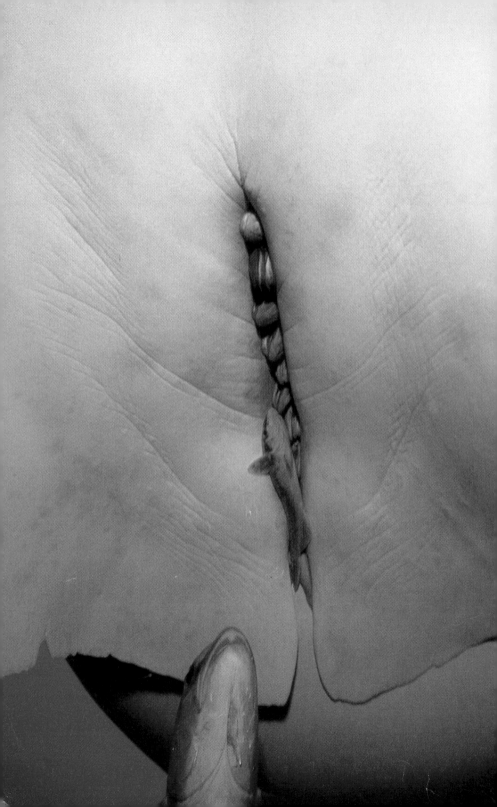

Chapter 3
Wonders and Mysteries

Whale sharks swim in warm, tropical waters near the earth's equator. Within that band, they really like to travel, following their food supplies as the plankton moves with warm ocean currents.

These huge sharks have been sighted in the Indian Ocean and in the Pacific Ocean off southern California and the Philippines. They are also found in the Gulf of Mexico and in the Ningaloo Reef off the coast of Australia.

Shore to Surface to Sea

Whale sharks swim on the surface. They also swim deep down in the water.

During the day, the hot tropical sun warms the water and drives the tiny plankton down as deep as 2,000 feet (600 meters). Whale sharks follow the plankton down into the depths. They come up to the surface in the evening, when the water cools. Scientists don't know how deep the shark will go. One diver followed a whale shark 40 feet (12 meters) down before turning back.

Whale sharks have been seen swimming near the shore, especially near coral reefs. But they are most often in the open sea.

Steady Cruisers

Whale sharks aren't known for fast swimming. They may not sprint, but they can really cruise. Big, slow beats of their powerful tails drive them forward, traveling at 3 to 5 miles (4.8 to 8 kilometers) an hour. Divers in boats have tried to keep up with them and failed.

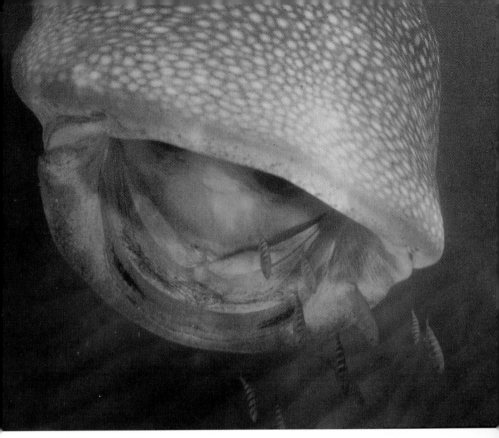

To feed, the whale shark just opens its mouth and swims. It doesn't need its teeth, which are small and harmless.

But the whale shark can also lie motionless in the water. Only the whale shark and the second-biggest shark, the basking shark, are able to do that. This ability is very unusual–all other sharks must keep swimming at all times to avoid sinking.

Whale sharks usually swim and feed alone, except while mating.

Mating and Giving Birth

Whale sharks are usually solitary swimmers. They swim alone. But they have also been seen in groups, or schools, with other whale sharks. They usually get together only when they mate.

Little is known about what happens when a female and a male whale shark meet and mate.

Actual mating has never been seen, although divers have seen whale sharks in what appeared to be mating behavior.

Male whale sharks, like other sharks, have two claspers–long, finlike structures on the ventral, or stomach side. In other sharks, one clasper is used to hold onto the female as they swim side by side. The other clasper is used to insert sperm into an opening on the female's stomach. Perhaps whale sharks do the same thing.

Eggs or Young?

Scientists are not certain whether these sharks lay eggs, as most sharks do, or give birth to living young. About two-thirds of all sharks give birth to live pups after eggs hatch inside the mother. Shark pups look just like miniature adult sharks. They are born ready to swim and hunt for food.

But some sharks lay eggs that hatch from egg cases. Egg cases are rectangular and look like little pillows. Sailors called them

The whale shark's mouth is at the front of its head, instead of underneath, as in most sharks.

"mermaids' purses." Egg cases have thin lines hanging off them. These lines get trapped in rocks on the ocean floor and hold the egg case steady and safe until the shark is born.

Until 1953, scientists didn't know which category whale sharks fit in. In that year, a shrimping boat working in the Gulf of Mexico off Texas brought up a huge egg case from 187 feet (57 meters) beneath the surface. It was 12 inches (30 centimeters) long and almost 6 inches (14 centimeters) wide. It was the biggest egg case ever seen.

Inside that huge egg case was a tiny spotted shark that looked just like an adult whale shark. Scientists now suspect that whale sharks lay eggs in egg cases, which hatch live baby sharks.

However, it is possible that an egg case containing a shark pup could be expelled, or aborted, before it was ready to be hatched inside the mother.

That's just one more mystery about whale sharks.

Chapter 4

Riding the Whale Sharks

Whale sharks are not afraid of people. Any fish as big as a whale shark doesn't have to fear anything!

But whale sharks do seem to be interested in people. A whale shark will let a diver grab hold of one of the long ridges on its back to ride along. When a whale shark has had enough of the human, it just turns tail and swims away—straight down. No human can keep up.

The Ride of Her Life

Dr. Eugenie Clark is one of the world's experts on sharks. She has also taken a total of 25 rides on whale sharks! The bigger a whale shark is, she says, the more tolerant of people it will be.

She says her first ride was the most thrilling. The ride on a 52-foot (16-meter) whale shark lasted four minutes. The huge fish swam down into the water and then back to the surface. According to Clark, it was like being on a living submarine.

On one ride, Clark grabbed onto a fin on the shark's back. Then she pulled her feet up and rode it the way a jockey rides a horse. Her arms tired as they whizzed along in the water. So she carefully let herself slip back to the tail. She hung on while the tail, which powers the shark's swimming, slapped her from side to side.

Finally, she let go and watched her living submarine disappear into the depths of the ocean.

Grabbing hold for a ride on a whale shark is an unforgettable experience.

Starring Roles

In 1926, filmmaker Mack Sennett tested a new underwater camera he had developed. He filmed a whale shark 65 feet (20 meters) long and 10 feet (3 meters) wide off the Gulf of California.

A huge whale shark makes this group of divers look like aquarium toys.

The first still photograph of a whale shark was taken in 1950 by photographer and diver Hans Hass. He just clicked away at a giant spotted shark he saw, not realizing that it was a whale shark.

Hass and a friend rode the shark's tail fin. It whipped them first left and then right. He signaled to his friend to hang on while he dropped back to shoot a picture of the ride.

Party Animal

Another diver described a shark that didn't want the fun to end. She said that seven divers spent three days riding a 33-foot (10-meter) female shark. After each dive, the shark followed the boat back toward the dock. Each day, the shark waited for the divers to return.

Whale sharks like to rub against floating objects. Scientists think they do this to rub parasites off their thick, elephant-like skin. One reason they might enjoy hitchhikers is because they help keep their skin clean.

Too Popular?

Scientists don't think that whale sharks are harmed by such riding games. But they are starting to worry about the sport becoming too popular.

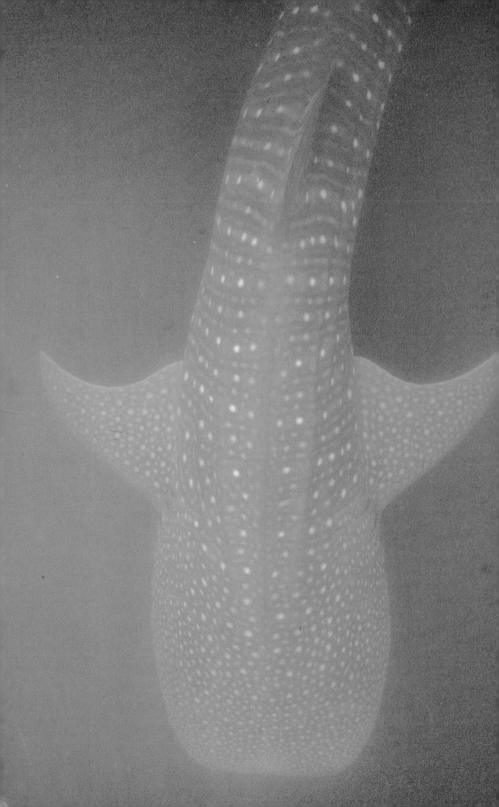

At one marine park, riding whale sharks has become a favorite tourist activity. Scientists worry that too much interaction with people might keep whale sharks away or cause them some kind of harm.

Although a whale shark is not going to attack a person who hitches a ride, the person can still be hurt. Sharks have very rough skin, with little, sharp points called denticles. These sharp points can seriously scrape the rider's skin if it is not protected.

Collision!

Whale sharks have had run-ins with ships. More than 20 collisions have been recorded. These big animals feed on the surface, moving slowly. They appear not to even notice when a ship approaches.

If a ship and a whale shark collide, it is the shark that usually loses out. The blow will kill it. However, smaller boats have been damaged by striking whale sharks.

A whale shark feeds near the surface as a boat keeps its distance.

Sharks and Humans

Despite these problems with ships, whale sharks have little to fear from humans. This is true for many reasons beyond their great size. Whale shark meat does not taste very good. Their teeth are too small to be useful as weapon points or jewelry. Many other sharks' teeth are used that way.

And whale sharks are hard to find and so large that hooking and killing them is more trouble than it's worth. Instead of fearing or killing them, humans prefer to play with them.

Humans have little to fear from whale sharks. Whale sharks seem to be interested in us. They don't seem to mind us hanging around them. They might even enjoy us. The worst

Undersea photographers have little to fear from the whale shark, except for its big, flapping tail.

that a whale shark has done to a human is to accidentally whack her or him with its tail. That can be quite a blow!

Luck and the Whale Shark

In Japanese lore, the whale shark is named for one of seven gods of good fortune. Japanese fishermen say that finding a whale shark is good luck. It means that there is lots of plankton around. And that means there are lots of plankton-eating fish around. Japanese fishermen don't want to kill this good luck charm.

To divers, whale sharks are good luck, too. The lucky few who have found them have enjoyed the most exciting rides of their lives.

Glossary

camouflage–color and patterns that make an animal hard to see against its background.

cartilage–hard but flexible material found in sharks instead of bones; humans have cartilage in their ears, noses, and kneecaps.

claspers–a pair of organs located on the abdomen of a male shark, used for mating. They look like extra fins.

gill slits–the long straight openings on the side of a shark into which water flows. A mako has five large gill slits.

keel–a flat part of the body that sticks out from another part, like the keel of a boat. A whale shark's keel strengthens its tail.

krill–tiny shrimp-like animals that float in the sea; an important part of plankton

mammals–animals that give birth to living young and produce milk to feed them. Humans and whales are mammals.

parasites–an animal that lives in or on another animal, feeding off it, and gradually harming it

plankton–the collection of tiny animals, especially krill, that swim in the ocean. Plankton is food to whale, basking, and megamouth sharks.

ventral–located on the stomach side of the shark, such as fins or claspers

To Learn More

Blassingame, Wyatt. *Wonders of Sharks.* New York: Dodd, Mead, and Co., 1984.

Cerullo, Mary M. *Sharks: Challengers of the Deep.* New York: Cobblehill Books, 1993.

Freedman, Russel. *Sharks.* New York: Holiday House, 1985.

Langley, Andrew. *The World of Sharks.* New York: Bookwright Press, 1987.

Springer Victor G. and Joy P. Gould. *Sharks In Question: The Smithsonian Answer Book.* 1989.

Steel, Rodney. *Sharks of the World.* New York: Facts on File, 1989.

Sharks, Silent Hunters of the Deep, Readers Digest, 1987.

About the Author

Anne Welsbacher is publications director at the Science Museum of Minnesota. She writes science articles for various publications and is a playwright.

Index